Once-a Ponce-a Time...

and other bean-isms

ONCE-A PONCE-A TIME...

and other bean-isms

by

ELLISON ROOKE

trillium memory books

2017

Printed in the United States of America

First Edition: January 2017

ISBN 978-0-9971549-7-9

Library of Congress Control Number: 2016959716

Published by
Trillium Memory Books
An imprint of redbat books
2901 Gekeler Lane
La Grande, OR 97850
www.TrilliumMemoryBooks.com

Text set in Century Gothic

All Artwork by Ellison Rooke

Book design by
Kristin Summers, redbat design
www.redbatdesign.com

"glikkum, glikkum, glikkum, glikkum, glikkum."

JUNE 2011
AGE 1

"scribbles"
magic marker, 2012

gravel = "***gabble!***"

MARCH 19, 2012
AGE $1^1/_2$

hiccups = "***hippup***"

MAY 5, 2012
AGE 2

The bean smacked her elbow on the gate, rubbed it a little and then tried to kiss it, herself.

JULY 24, 2012
AGE 2

dandelion =
"***dandy-lion-lion-lion-lion-lion-lion...***"

AUGUST 28, 2012
AGE 2

"outside, me?!"
or "cookies, want me!"
or "in da car, you."

Toddlers are like little Yodas.

OCTOBER 5, 2012
AGE 2

When the bean woke up
this morning, she smiled and said,
"i **missed** you, mama!"

OCTOBER 11, 2012
AGE 2

In bean-speak,
Halloween is all about
carving "***puppins***" and
saying "***tricky-treat***!"

OCTOBER 31, 2012
AGE 2

Mama just spent the last ten minutes in the grocery store, pushing around one of those carts with the kid's car in the front. It's unknown how everyone else felt, but we think that a two-year-old yelling, "i ***dry-bing***, mama!" the entire time was awesome.

NOVEMBER 17, 2012
AGE 2

"i *yub* you, mama.
you so pwitty.
you so BOO-ti-foll!"

"Aw... thanks Beanie,"
Mama says.
"You're going to make me cry."

"no, you gonna
make **me** cry, mama."

DECEMBER 17, 2012
AGE $2^1/_2$

"i *yub* you **too much**, mama!"

JANUARY 2, 2013
AGE 2 1/2

The bean made Mama sign
her Valentine card
for Daddy as
"to Mechagodzilla,
love Godzilla!"

Needless to say, he loved it.

FEBRUARY 14, 2013
AGE 2½

While Mama was taking a shower this morning, the bean kept opening the door every few minutes to yell, "mama! what **happening** in dare?!"

MARCH 1, 2013
AGE $2^1/_2$

At the park, the bean finally
worked up the courage
to talk to another little girl
and proudly said,
"hi! i'm ***Simba***!"

MARCH 10, 2013
AGE $2^1/_2$

Every time Mama asks the bean
to pick up a pile of toys
that have been splayed about,
the bean looks her straight
in the eye and says,
"but... it's a ***party***!"

APRIL 6, 2013
AGE 2½

Daddy was listing off foods for the bean to choose from, one of which he purposely mispronounced as "blueberries and *kwi-no-uh*." The bean scrunched her eyebrows and said, all exasperated-like, "it's **keen-wah**, daddy."

APRIL 10, 2013
AGE $2^{1}/_{2}$

There are always many sweet moments in our days, but today's sweetest so far is this: the bean climbing up onto the couch next to Mama, gently grasping one of her curls and saying, "i just want to hold your hair, mama."

APRIL 20, 2013
AGE $2^1/_2$

Out of the blue, the bean just declared, "i want to fly...all by myself!" Then, with a trembling chin, she burst into tears, crying out, "i want to ***FLYYYYY***!"

APRIL 24, 2013
AGE 2½

There's something really precious about a two-year-old following her dad around and saying (in her tiny, li'l voice): "i **love** you, dr. octopus!"

MAY 5, 2013
AGE 2 1/2

"...but i want HULK pancakes, not mickey mouse!"

MAY 10, 2013
AGE $2^1/_2$

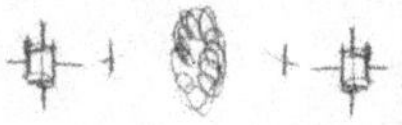

The bean with a squirt gun:
"i'm-a squirt this chair...
i'm-a squirt the garage door...
i'm-a squirt this flower...
...my shoes...
...these rocks...
...this grass...
...this cat...
no, THIS cat..."
and finally,
"i, i, i, i'm-a squirt the
moooooooooon, mama!"

MAY 20, 2013
AGE 2 1/2

Today the bean asked,
"where is daddy's dad?
where is daddy's mom?"
then, of course,
"where is *your* dad, mama?"
and "where is *your* mom?"
After the other explanations,
Mama got a bit weepy and
said, "Well, my mom isn't here
anymore. She... she died."
The bean paused a moment and
then hugged her, saying,
"she gonna be OK, mama...
she only a ***yiddle bit*** died."

JULY 5, 2013
AGE 3

Mama asked the bean if she
could stand on one foot.
She said "yep!"
and promptly stomped
her left foot on top
of her right.

JULY 23, 2013
AGE 3

Mama:
"Say goodbye to the lake."

the bean:
"but, where is it *going*?"

AUGUST 2, 2013
AGE 3

We bought the bean
a fun gift today:
she's very much enjoying her
"***walkie-hockey-talkies***."

NOVEMBER 17, 2013
AGE 3

Mama:
"Hey beanie,
what would you like
for dinner?

the bean:
"**i'm drawing!!**
don't talk to me."

DECEMBER 1, 2013
AGE 3 1/2

"please, mama?
pretty please
with **pepper** on top?!"

DECEMBER 11, 2013
AGE 3$^{1}/_{2}$

Daddy to the bean (jokingly):
"do you want a taste
of my beer?"

the bean:
"no!! i'm little and **cute**."

DECEMBER 13, 2013
AGE 3½

In a whisper,
the bean just said to Mama,
"your face is nice."

DECEMBER 14, 2013
AGE 3½

The bean helped wrap
and decorate a Christmas gift
for Daddy, but she was a
little too excited to show him.
Mama had barely placed it
under the tree when the bean
grabbed Daddy's face with both
hands, looked him straight
in the eye and said,
"daddy! it's a **book**!
it's a book about...**cereal**!!
you're gonna ***yub*** it!"

DECEMBER 24, 2013
AGE 3½

"it's hungry, ***humpy*** hippo!"

DECEMBER 25, 2013
AGE $3^1/_2$

The bean's idea of writing "a really big" letter *E* is to draw a vertical line with lots of horizontal "arms."

JANUARY 2, 2014
AGE 3 1/2

the bean:
"hold onto me, princess!
i'll save you!"

Mama:
"Wait. *I'm* the princess? But, *you*
should be the princess.

the bean:
"no, *you're* the princess because
you have long hair."

JANUARY 11, 2014
AGE 3 1/2

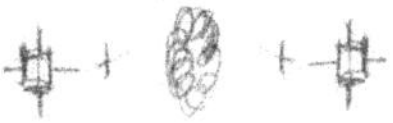

The best thing about
the bean learning to spell
is that she sees the letter *E*
everywhere and says, excitedly,
"i saw my name, mama!
my ***name***!"

JANUARY 31, 2014
AGE $3^1/_2$

While playing hide-and-seek with Mama, the bean searched and searched but was soon frustrated. She got quiet and sad and then said to Daddy, "i can't find my mama... i miss her."

FEBRUARY 4, 2014
AGE $3^1/_2$

Once-a Ponce-a Time...and other bean-isms

The bean likes to sit underneath tables and she did so today at a restaurant. Within 30 seconds, however, she jumped out and said, "i can't **handle** all this gum!"

FEBRUARY 11, 2014
AGE 3½

After repeatedly asking
to have a book read to her
in the car, and hearing the
response every time as
"I can't right now, sweetie,
I'm driving," the bean whined,
"**mommm**, every time you drive,
you don't know how to read!"

FEBRUARY 23, 2014
AGE $3^1/_2$

"row-row-row your boat
get me down your stream
merry-merry-merry-merry
it was all a dream."

FEBRUARY 27, 2014
AGE 3 1/2

"let's play
hide-and-sneak!"

FEBRUARY 27, 2014
AGE 3 1/2

the costumed bean: "my spidey sense is rumbling!"

MARCH 14, 2014
AGE $3^1/_2$

After eating a chewy candy,
the bean says,
"they make my cheek wrinkle!"

APRIL 3, 2014
AGE $3^1/_2$

As the bean studies her new
watercolor palette, Mama says,
"Can you name all of those
colors for me?"

the bean:
"sure! there's *hellboy...*
his girlfriend...
wolverine...
toadie..."

APRIL 3, 2014
AGE 3½

"you can sit next to me, mama...
and you can take a nap
on my shoulder!"

APRIL 17, 2014
AGE 3½

"*once-a ponce-a time...*"

APRIL 20, 2014
AGE 3$^{1}/_{2}$

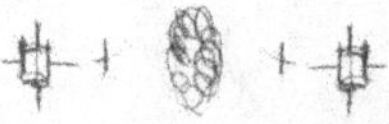

In her sleep this morning,
the bean whined a little
and then said:
"...but i'm ***godzilla***!"

APRIL 20, 2014
AGE 3½

There's nothing quite like getting frustrated with the internet and having your three-year-old say, "you just have to be **patient**, mama!"

MAY 15, 2014
AGE $3^1/_2$

"i want a baby ***brudder*** to come in the mailbox!"

MAY 16, 2014
AGE 3 1/2

Talking about kids at her school,
the bean says,
"i was playing with Ollie,
and then he went to go play with
some ***other characters***."

MAY 16, 2014
AGE 3 1/2

Again, talking about school, she described one of her classmates as "***a naughty character***."

MAY 16, 2014
AGE 3 1/2

the bean:
"what character are you, mama?"

Mama:
"Um... I'll be Hulk."

the bean:
"oh, ok! ...because you're so **chubby**?"

MAY 17, 2014
AGE 3 1/2

wallet = "***wallop***"
as in, "mom! i put your wallop
on the counter."

MAY 28, 2014
AGE 4

Trying to comfort Mama,
the bean gives her a huge hug
and says, "there...
that will feel you better!"

JUNE 5, 2014
AGE 4

"let's go eat some people and let's go find some werewolf food!"

JUNE 5, 2014
AGE 4

Daddy:
"Hey Bean, do you think you could draw me a picture of a werewolf?"

the bean:
"no... i can't, because i only have **paws**."

JUNE 5, 2014
AGE 4

the bean:
" *cough* *cough* *cough* "

Daddy:
"Are you ok?!"

the bean:
"yes. i had a
werewolf hairball."

JUNE 5, 2014
AGE 4

As the bean tries to wrestle
with her dad, he asks,
"What are you doing?!"
She responds with,
"i'm ***werewolfing***!"

JUNE 5, 2014
AGE 4

"that just scared
the ***creep*** outta me!"

JUNE 9, 2014
AGE 4

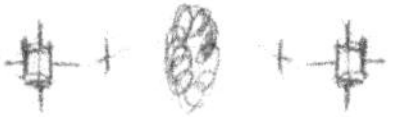

"i love you mama!
you're so cute and sweet and
fun. you're like a little rat.
a little baby rat.
from a little rat family.

...and they lived happily
ever after.

there. that's a little nibble
of a story."

JUNE 10, 2014
AGE 4

the bean:
"what was that sound?!"

Mama:
"Just the printer. I had to print
something out."

the bean:
"oh. i thought it was
my ***beanie-sense***.
i have that, y'know."

JUNE 17, 2014
AGE 4

"when i spin around and around,
it makes me soooo ***bizzy***!"

JUNE 27, 2014
AGE 4

"i'm not beanie.
i'm Will Smith."

JUNE 28, 2014
AGE 4

"mama!
i'm gonna ***attackle*** you!!"

JULY 2, 2014
AGE 4

"daddy, you need
to go to time out.
that means you
can't play baseball
or do dishes."

JULY 2, 2014
AGE 4

"when i grow up, i wanna have dark skin and drive a car!"

JULY 3, 2014
AGE 4

The bean has a stack of plastic disks from CD-R spindles that she uses as her pretend music CDs. One of them broke today and Daddy said it needed to be thrown away. She sighed and then said, sadly, "but it was a **really** good song."

JULY 8, 2014
AGE 4

The bean was scratching
the cushion on the piano bench
over and over.
Suddenly, she stopped.

Daddy:
"That was really cool.
Keep doing it!"

the bean:
"i can't. i'm not a
werewolf anymore!"

JULY 8, 2014
AGE 4

Today, in all seriousness, and with much enthusiasm, the bean called a watermelon slice "***water-on-the-cob!***"

JULY 9, 2014
AGE 4

Mama started to pour some cereal into a bowl and the bean stopped her, saying, "no. i can do it by my *own* self, cuz i'm a ***genius***!"

JULY 16, 2014
AGE 4

Mama:
"That's called a *daddy-long-leg*."

the bean:
"really? is there a ***mama-long-leg*** and a ***beanie-long-leg***?"

JULY 18, 2014
AGE 4

Daddy:
"Hey Bean, do you know what starts tonight? A whole new season of *FaceOff* with all new contestants and make-up and everything!"

the bean:
"you're blowing...
my mind..."

JULY 22, 2014
AGE 4

A message from the bean
to actor Will Smith:

"sometimes i pretend
to be you
and sometimes i pretend
to be Jaden.
i know things can be
frus-ter-ating, but i'm gonna
make the world better."

JULY 25, 2014
AGE 4

While acting out a
scenario from a kid's TV show:
"baby jaguar, look!
it's a ***rat-ronna-saurus rex***!"

JULY 28, 2014
AGE 4

"i'm having a
sneezy problem."

AUGUST 2, 2014
AGE 4

"you smell like beer and jam in a dirty shoe."

AUGUST 4, 2014
AGE 4

While at the store, Mama asked which mac & cheese box to get, "shells or regular?" The bean pointed right away to the regular box and responded with, "the smiley faces!"

AUGUST 5, 2014
AGE 4

Mama:
"Are you ok?"

the bean:
"yeah... (rubbing her nose).
i'm just trying to keep my nose
from ***bless-you-ing***."

SEPTEMBER 1, 2014
AGE 4

After returning from her
grandmother's house,
the bean announced (excitedly):
"i met one of Oma's friends!!"

Daddy:
"Really? How'd that go?"

the bean (disappointedly):
"um... she was **old**, too."

SEPTEMBER 4, 2014
AGE 4

"you can be a monster
if you want to!"

SEPTEMBER 4, 2014
AGE 4

After eating a cookie, the bean rushes into the kitchen and heads straight for the trash can, where she brushes off some crumbs. "i had to come in here," she says, "because I had a big mess of ***crumbles***!"

OCTOBER 23, 2014
AGE 4

Mama:
"Maybe for your first haircut,
we could find a
kids' haircutting place."

A wee bit horrified, the bean
paused and then asked:
"you mean **kids**
would cut my hair?!"

OCTOBER 29, 2014
AGE 4

Daddy was talking with the bean about a book of his that she wanted to keep, and he asked her what she would do with it. Pointing at her bookshelves, she said, "well, I'll keep it in my little ***book land***!"

OCTOBER 29, 2014
AGE 4

Wanting to play a song for Daddy
on her guitar, the bean asked
for a pick. After receiving one,
she began singing,
"*pick, pick, picky...*"
Then, in full deadpan mode,
"...i'm a **picky** eater."

OCTOBER 29, 2014
AGE 4

Now that it's dark when we get up in the morning for school, it's a bit confusing to the bean. This morning, she sleepily asked, "you mean... i have to go to school **at night**?!"

OCTOBER 29, 2014
AGE 4

Went to the tap room again today for some growlers of beer and the bean called it "***the beer hotel.***"

NOVEMBER 1, 2014
AGE 4

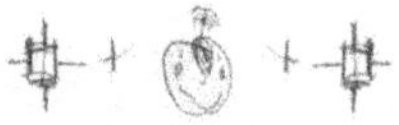

While playing a video game with Daddy, each player had a skateboard that left behind a colored path—Daddy had red and the bean had blue. After playing for awhile, the bean said, "check out my ***blue***-*ness*!"

NOVEMBER 4, 2014
AGE 4

Trying to describe
a silent movie,
the bean called it a
"***quiet film***."

NOVEMBER 27, 2014
AGE 4 1/2

nutcracker = "***nutcutter***"

NOVEMBER 30, 2014
AGE $4^1/_2$

Grandma K and the bean
were trying to get something out
from under the bed, but they
couldn't reach it, so Grandma
suggested using a broom.
The bean paused, then said,
"but... a broom
doesn't have **hands**!"

DECEMBER 21, 2014
AGE 4 1/2

While watching TV, the bean sees a commercial for some sort of moisturizer and then yells excitedly to Mama:
"i want you to get some of that. it makes you **younger**!!"

JANUARY 25, 2015
AGE 4½

While out driving this morning,
we had to pull over to let a
Sheriff's truck pass.

the bean:
"mom! i saw **lights**!"

Mama:
"Crazy, huh? Something's going
on so he has to hurry and
get there. What do you
think happened?"

the bean:
"i think maybe somebody said a
really, really, ***really*** bad word!"

JANUARY 30, 2015
AGE 4 1/2

"i gave my cold to my dad,
but i'm **still** sick!"

FEBRUARY 4, 2015
AGE 4 1/2

While watching a basketball game, the bean blurts out, "they just said the Warriors have to go to **time out**!"

FEBRUARY 22, 2015
AGE 4 1/2

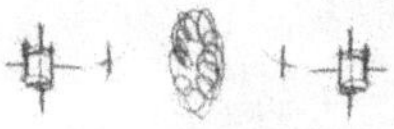

Walking through a local cemetery, the bean says: "mom! it's like a land of **zombies**!"

FEBRUARY 22, 2015
AGE 4 1/2

While eating meatloaf,
the bean runs out of ketchup and
asks for more "***makeup***."

FEBRUARY 24, 2015
AGE 4 1/2

the bean: "mom? do baby cats turn into *kid* cats?"

Mama: "Yes."

the bean: "do kid cats turn into *grown-up* cats?"

Mama: "Yes."

the bean: "do grown-up cats turn into *old* cats?

Mama: "Yes."

the bean: "and... old cats turn into **zombies**!"

MARCH 18, 2015
AGE 4 1/2

"i just had a ***remember-y***!"

APRIL 14, 2015
AGE 4 1/2

"bust my **brains**! this is fruitier than chocolate!"

APRIL 15, 2015
AGE $4^1/_2$

"i miss my ***baby-ness***..."

MAY 20, 2015
AGE 4 1/2

the bean:
"look at my drawing.
this is what i saw!"

Mama & Daddy:
"What do you mean?
You saw it in your dreams?"

the bean:
"no. i saw it in my ***imaginarious***."

MAY 25, 2015
AGE 4 1/2

Mama:
"Today is the last day before you turn five!"

the bean:
"oh... (pouting a bit), but i'm gonna **miss** being four."

MAY 25, 2015
AGE 4 1/2

"mom! the cricket outside
is singing you
a birthday song!"

MAY 31, 2015
AGE 5

seasoning = "*sneeze-oning*"
as in: "please don't put any
sneeze-oning on my
mac & cheese."

JUNE 3, 2015
AGE 5

"do you know why i want a little brother? so when we grow up, he can be my husband!"

JUNE 10, 2015
AGE 5

the bean:
"do you find interest in that guy?"

Mama:
"What do you mean?"

the bean:
"do... you... find...
in-ter-est... in... him?"

Mama:
"Uh... sure? I guess I'm still not
quite sure what you're asking."

the bean (clearly exasperated):
"**mom! do you think he's *hot*?!**"

JUNE 10, 2015
AGE 5

"what did the pea
say to the other pea?

...nothing. haha!"

JUNE 12, 2015
AGE 5

"um, dad?
that guy on the radio just said
that Miles Davis is **blue**!"

JUNE 13, 2015
AGE 5

"i wanted to write *mom* because i didn't know how to spell your name."

JUNE 14, 2015
AGE 5

Mama:
"Uh-oh. i think i caught
your cold."

the bean:
"no. i still have mine.
you caught your **own** cold."

JUNE 14, 2015
AGE 5

The bean became a bit obsessed with photos of a professional basketball player's son, who is almost exactly one year older than she is. Mama told the bean that perhaps she might marry him one day, and the bean responded by rolling her eyes, throwing her arms in the air, and saying, "but mom, i don't even know where he **lives**!"

JUNE 14, 2015
AGE 5

The bean called Mama on the intercom and declared, "mom! guess what? i'm playing ***chest***! ...i mean... mom! guess what? i'm playing ***CHESS***!"

JUNE 23, 2015
AGE 5

badminton = "*birdnet*"
as in, "dad, can we
play ***birdnet***?"

JULY 2, 2015
AGE 5

"i drew a ***mow-lawner***!"

JULY 3, 2015
AGE 5

"that's a TV, and that's the TV ***hold-upper***."

JULY 3, 2015
AGE 5

Using her Avengers toy cell
phone, the bean dialed
a number and said,
"hello, Santa?"
Then,
"no, no, no, n—**wait**!
don't hang up!"

JULY 20, 2015
AGE 5

While playing video games with Daddy, they both start talkin' smack. The bean's contribution? "how's your meatball doin' in that **oven**??! haha!"

JULY 28, 2015
AGE 5

First thing, when the bean
woke up this morning,
she opened her eyes and said,
"oh. well, **that**
didn't take long."

"What didn't take long?"
Mama asked.

"morning."

JULY 28, 2015
AGE 5

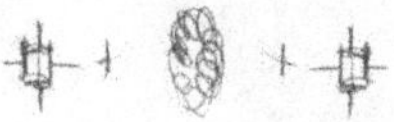

Playing her guitar,
the bean sweetly says,
"my first song
was called *walking*.
my second song
was called *friday cat*.
and now..."
(deepens her voice
and scrunches her face),
"this one is called,
death of hell!"

JULY 31, 2015
AGE 5

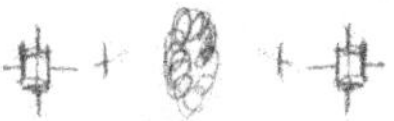

"geesh.
i'm sweating like a **bird**!"

AUGUST 1, 2015
AGE 5

the bean loves playing "***goose-goose-duck***"

AUGUST 3, 2015
AGE 5

Mama asked the bean
if she wanted to sleep with
one of her stuffed animals
and she said, "no, mama,
you're my animal."

AUGUST 6, 2015
AGE 5

Waving around a drawing,
the bean says,
"it's *you*, mama! and this is
your pet... a dog.
he looks like an alien because
i was trying to draw four legs
and i got a little carried away."

AUGUST 10, 2015
AGE 5

Having watched numerous
"out of the box" videos together
online, we heard her in the next
room today explaining
(to no one) what the pieces of
her new toy set were... in detail.
Although no camera was around,
she exclaimed,
"i'm making a video!!!"

AUGUST 10, 2015
AGE 5

Exactly one piece of lettuce =
"***salad***"

AUGUST 15, 2015
AGE 5

salad dressing = "***lettuce sauce***"

AUGUST 15, 2015
AGE 5

The areas behind your knees?
Those are called "***leg pits***."

AUGUST 22, 2015
AGE 5

Although she had fun during her first day of kindergarten yesterday and had her outfit and lunch planned out for today, the bean was less than enthusiastic about getting up early this morning.

When she found out that she would also be missing her favorite new show, she sadly looked at Daddy and said, "i don't want this job anymore."

SEPTEMBER 3, 2015
AGE 5

While talking about her second
day of kindergarten,
the bean said, forlornly,
"my classroom is too small.
there's no room for me!"
We assumed that she meant
there were more students
attending than there were on the
first day, and therefore, she'd had
to sit with more kids at her table.
Nope. The reason was actually
"because i can't even **lay down**!"

SEPTEMBER 4, 2015
AGE 5

While putting on her Indiana Jones costume, the bean called herself "***andy-andy jones***."

SEPTEMBER 13, 2015
AGE 5

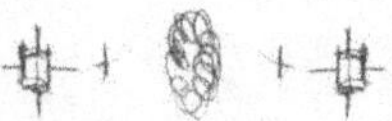

Mama (yawning):
"...I don't know why I'm
so *tired* today!"

the bean:
"because you're **old** and
sometimes it makes you tired."

SEPTEMBER 20, 2015
AGE 5

"look mom! i can do push-ups
and ***jumpy-jacks***!"

SEPTEMBER 23, 2015
AGE 5

As Mama and the bean
walked on either side
of a pole, the bean said,
"mom? will you be my butter
and i'll be the bread?"

SEPTEMBER 25, 2015
AGE 5

"if we had a little ***mow-lawner***,
i could ***mow-lawn*** the yard when
it needs to be ***mow-lawned***!"

SEPTEMBER 25, 2015
AGE 5

"you just hit me in
the ***privates*** of my neck."

SEPTEMBER 25, 2015
AGE 5

Looking through a selection of movies, the bean asks, "is that one ***Peter Pants***?"

OCTOBER 5, 2015
AGE 5

The bean was filling out a form that asked for her three biggest mistakes. She wrote two statements down and then asked for help on the third. Daddy said, "What about talking back to your mom?" Without hesitation, she lifted one eyebrow and said, "uh... that **wasn't** a mistake."

OCTOBER 16, 2015
AGE 5

While watching our
veggie pizza being prepared,
Mama said, "Mmmm...
doesn't that look yummy?"
The bean replied with a very dry,
"no. i don't like ***leaves***."

NOVEMBER 4, 2015
AGE 5

All three of us were sitting on the
couch, quietly watching TV.
Out of nowhere,
the bean asked, "have i ever
pooped in my pants?"
Laughing, Daddy said,
"Uh... no. Not since you
stopped wearing diapers.
What made you ask that?"
She replied,
"well, nobody was
saying anything!"

NOVEMBER 4, 2015
AGE 5

As we were getting ready to go to a Christmas bazaar where they serve fresh donuts, the bean kept referring to it as "***the donut festival***."

NOVEMBER 7, 2015
AGE 5

"i'm having a ***daze-a voo*** again"

NOVEMBER 26, 2015
AGE $5^1/_2$

Wistfully, the bean
just sighed and said,
"i wish i could get money for
picking my nose."

NOVEMBER 26, 2015
AGE $5^1/_2$

"i'm gonna go practice
my bat-a-rang skills."

NOVEMBER 28, 2015
AGE 5 1/2

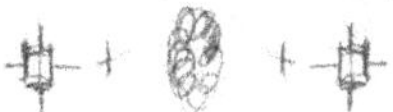

Went to a church bazaar today and now the bean keeps referring to it as "that ***bizarro*** thing."

DECEMBER 5, 2015
AGE 5 1/2

Looking at the clouds
moving in the sky:
"mom! the clouds are
running away!"

DECEMBER 9, 2015
AGE 5 1/2

After watching *Home Alone*
for the first time (and loving it!),
the bean now asks often,
"can we watch one of the
I'm Alone movies?!"

DECEMBER 9, 2015
AGE 5 1/2

Seeing a character in a movie who realizes that he has itchy, red spots all over his body, the bean yells out, "i know! he has the ***chicken spots***!"

DECEMBER 9, 2015
AGE 5 1/2

Mistakenly combining
cell phone, *selfie*, and *selfish*,
the bean tells Mama,
"i'm making a call
on my ***cellfish***."

DECEMBER 18, 2015
AGE $5^1/_2$

The bean sings
Rudolph and includes,
"won't you ***glide*** my
sleigh tonight."

DECEMBER 20, 2015
AGE $5^1/_2$

Daddy leaned over the bean,
who was sitting at the table
and she took a big whiff
of his armpit. She paused
and then said,
"smells like **work**."

DECEMBER 21, 2015
AGE 5 1/2

Daddy said,
"how ya like dem apples?"
and the bean replied,
"i don't like the taste of ***green***."

DECEMBER 26, 2015
AGE $5^1/_2$

Mama leaned down
to hug the bean,
who was curled into a ball
on the floor. As she did so, her hair
fell down over both of them.
"wait!" the bean yelled.
"not like that. you're making
my head go ***dark***!"

DECEMBER 27, 2015
AGE 5 1/2

"i just took a teeny nap—
a ***mouse nap***!"

JANUARY 6, 2016
AGE 5 1/2

Mama:
"Wow, Beanie.
You just read those two
movie posters by yourself.
Great job!"

the bean:
"and now, i'm gonna read...
your mind!"

JANUARY 12, 2016
AGE $5^1/_2$

"i love my toy army men.
i *died* for them for
my birthday!"

JANUARY 20, 2016
AGE 5½

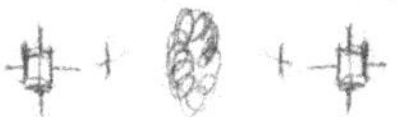

While watching a show about electric eels, the narrator made a statement about the amount of voltage it would take to "kill a grown man." The bean turned to Daddy and asked, "but... would it kill a grown-up **girl**?"

FEBRUARY 15, 2016
AGE 5½

While discussing really cold weather, the bean declared, "like in *arc-**ANT**-ica*!"

FEBRUARY 17, 2016
AGE 5 1/2

"eenie-meenie-minee-moe
uh...
cut a spider's leg off...
my...
mom...
said...
you are...
not...
it!"

FEBRUARY 22, 2016
AGE 5 1/2

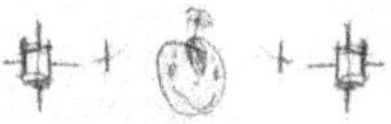

After visiting with her
li'l bestie, Juliette,
who was selling Girl Scout
cookies, the bean asked,
"um... when i get older,
can i sell **boy** scout cookies?"

MARCH 12, 2016
AGE 5 1/2

Daddy:
"Um, who was the last to use this Scotch tape? It's all messed up. Was it *you*, junior?"

the bean:
"yes, but my name's not ***junior***.

Daddy:
"Well it is right now."

the bean:
"oh no... is that my ***in-trouble*** name?"

MARCH 12, 2016
AGE 5 1/2

Instead of saying that her foot is asleep, the bean says, "my foot is ***tired***!"

MAY 6, 2016
AGE 5 1/2

the bean:
"can i have some of those
rolling stones?"

Daddy and Mama both chuckle
and say, "Um... what?"

the bean:
"y'know... that cereal?
the ***stones***?

Us: silence.
and then, "Do you mean...
Cocoa Pebbles?"

the bean:
"yes!"

MAY 10, 2016
AGE 5 1/2

Daddy:
"What kind of music is this, Bean?"

the bean:
"um... it's ***home music***."

Daddy (proudly):
"Yes! It's *house music*!"

MAY 22, 2016
AGE 5½

hugging + snuggling = "*huggling*"
as in, "mama! i missed you
so much! we have to do
some ***huggling***!!"

JUNE 9, 2016
AGE 6

Whispering in Mama's ear,
the bean said, "mama!
i wish we had a whole lotta
money because then
we could go buy a little
brother or sister...
and i would pick a **sister**!"

JUNE 28, 2016
AGE 6

Dungeon-crawler style
video games will now be known
as "***under-crawlers***."

JUNE 30, 2016
AGE 6

"ew! that's disgusting!
it smells like...
like ***old people's fingers***!"

JULY 2, 2016
AGE 6

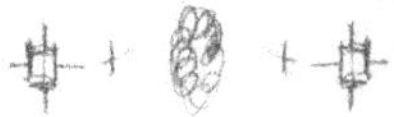

Daddy gave the bean
a true but long, drawn-out
explanation of Independence
Day and she was a great sport—
paying very close attention and
nodding at the appropriate times.
Just to be sarcastic, Mama asked
her to explain what Daddy had
just said. The bean responded,
very matter-of-factly with,
"i can't, because it all got lost
inside a tube in my head."

JULY 4, 2016
AGE 6

While at a restaurant, the bean repeatedly inched toward the kids' area, but would quickly—and sadly—come back to the table each time. Realizing that all of the other kids were actually toddlers and much younger than the bean, Mama asked her what was wrong. Without hesitation the bean frowned and replied with, "***hashtag: goo-goo ga-ga***."

JULY 14, 2016
AGE 6

After talking about Mt. St. Helens
and other volcanoes,
the bean asked,
"do we have volcanoes *here*?"

Mama:
"Well, Mt. Hood is actually
a volcano but it's dormant...
kind of like it's sleeping."

the bean (with a worried look):
"if we make a **really** loud noise,
will we wake it up?!"

AUGUST 7, 2016
AGE 6

"i really want a pet ***blutter-fy***."

AUGUST 19, 2016
AGE 6

After listening to lots of gibberish and goofiness from the bean, Daddy said, "You're delirious." Without missing a beat, she said, "no. you mean ***hilarious***!"

SEPTEMBER 9, 2016
AGE 6

"i don't want
to ***parcipitate***."

SEPTEMBER 11, 2016
AGE 6

Out of the blue, the bean asks, "is it flowers and guns? or guns and flowers?"

It took us a second, but then we caught up and had to tell her that, actually, the band's name is *Guns 'n' Roses*.

SEPTEMBER 13, 2016
AGE 6

"there are **three** Ariannas
at my school:
Arianna, *Arianna*, and...
oh! *Arianna*."

SEPTEMBER 19, 2016
AGE 6

"i threw that ball, like, 45 feet!
well... maybe 45 ***fingers***."

SEPTEMBER 26, 2016
AGE 6

"i miss yesterday."

SEPTEMBER 27, 2016
AGE 6

The bean was chosen as the
"Star Student of the Week"
and has been able to bring
something each day
for *show-and-tell*.
Tonight, she exclaimed,
"i know what i want to bring
for tomorrow. i want to
bring **you**, mama!!"

SEPTEMBER 28, 2016
AGE 6

"mom? while we're snuggling, can you put on my pajamas for me?"

OCTOBER 5, 2016
AGE 6

Mama quickly put her hair up to get it out of her face and the bean said, disapprovingly, "mom, really? ...a **man bun**?"

OCTOBER 13, 2016
AGE 6

Daddy was introducing the bean to coffee cake and she asked, "*coffee cake*? but... is it ok for **kids**?"

OCTOBER 21, 2016
AGE 6

"i'm just a **kid**!
a tiny ol' kid..."

OCTOBER 23, 2016
AGE 6

"eating"
wax crayon, 2012

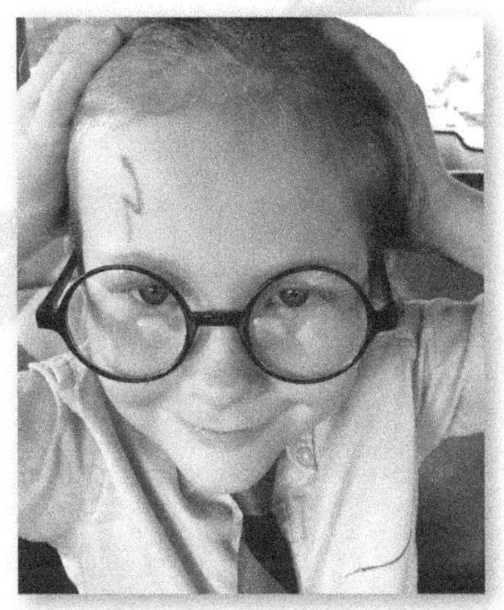

ABOUT THE AUTHOR

Possessed with red hair and blue eyes,
Ellison Rooke is a left-handed illustrator,
a natural storyteller, a painter,
a writer, a poet and a rapper,
an ambidextrous athlete,
a mathematician, and an
aspiring entomologist.

This is her first book of insight, questions,
and humorous observations.

www.EllisonRooke.com

For more information,
or to order additional copies,
please visit our website:

www.TrilliumMemoryBooks.com

www.ingramcontent.com/pod-product-compliance
Lightning Source LLC
Chambersburg PA
CBHW051726040426
42447CB00008B/992

* 9 7 8 0 9 9 7 1 5 4 9 7 9 *